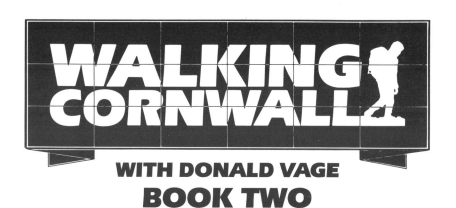

WITH DONALD VAGE
BOOK TWO

FOURTEEN CORNISH COUNTRYSIDE & COASTAL WALKS – INCLUDING THE SAINTS' WAY – WITH MAPS & PHOTOGRAPHS

First published in Great Britain 1989

Reprinted by Cornwall Books 1993

Copyright © Westcountry Books 1993

ISBN 1 871060 20 6

British Library Cataloguing-in-Publication Data
CIP Data for this book is available from the British Library

CORNWALL BOOKS
An imprint of Westcountry Books

Sales and Publishing

Westcountry Books
Unit 1 Chinon Court
Lower Moor Way
Tiverton
Devon EX16 6SS
Tel: 0884 243242
Fax: 0884 243325

Printed and bound in Great Britain by BPCC Wheatons Ltd

BOOK TWO
CONTENTS

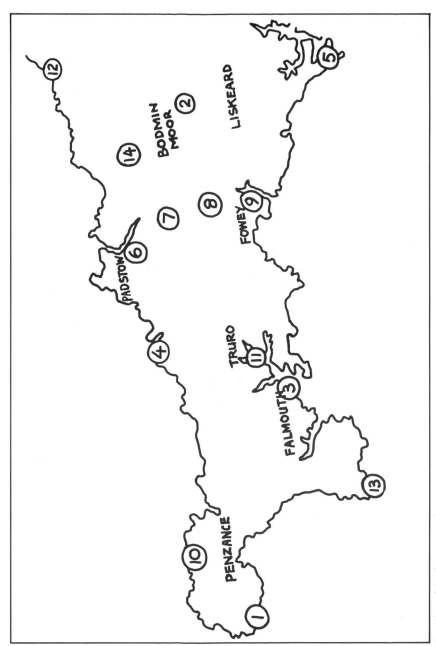

Location of the fourteen walks.

FOREWORD

So to my second attempt at sharing with you the pleasures that my wife and I, and Tessa our dachshund, find in walking in our beloved Cornwall. There are walks for all seasons, and I have tried to vary inland routes with coastal and moorland scenery to suit the mood.

Not all the walks are circular, but if I can find an alternative return route, I will certainly take it. I also have the family unit very much in mind as I write, suggesting where the very young and very old might meet up with the active walkers.

The same basic suggestions are on offer: good boots, maps and compass, emergency rations and clothes, and a deep respect for the Country Code and other people's property.

It will soon become obvious that this book, like Book One, is intended for those who enjoy 'a good day out', either alone or *en famille* and who do not expect the author to be a specialist or expert on any particular subject (which he is not).

The greatest pleasure I have received over the publication of Book One is the now known certainty that it encouraged many others to enjoy walks in areas that they did not know before and that my general instructions had been varied enormously, as I wished they would be. The rather sketchy maps that appear in both volumes are only intended as rough guides and, as before, I hope readers will feel able to vary them to suit their own inclinations. However, I would heartily recommend using the Ordnance Survey 1:50,000 maps (or the even more detailed 1:25,000 series) so as to avoid straying from public rights of way in open country.

A message that has come across, also, is that sometimes, because of time or physical disability, a shorter walk would be welcome and you will see that this book does include a few short 'strolls'. (It becomes easier to devise these as I approach my seventieth birthday.) For the hardier walker I have also included the popular Saints' Way walk from Padstow to Fowey – divided into four reasonably easy stages.

I wish I knew who wrote these lines as they are so close to my own philosophy:

Yet, further, you never enjoy the world ought, 'till you so love the beauty of enjoying it that you are covetous and earnest to persuade others to enjoy it.

DONALD VAGE

(21 April 1988. Today I heard the cuckoo on Bodmin Moor from the top of Alex Tor and yesterday I found two miles of paths, unknown to me before, beside the West Looe River: Happy Days!)

WALK ONE

A cross-country walk to a high coastal vantage point, a quiet fishing cove and a holy well.
AROUND GWENNAP HEAD
OS Map (1:50,000) 203.
Length: approximately three or six miles.

We begin this first walk at the little church of St Levan, nestling cosily in a hollow, allowing the prevailing Atlantic gales to blow over and around its protecting hill. Beside the church is a field which acts as a car-park (approached from Porthcurno and past the Minack Theatre entrance). It is useful to know about when you want to visit Porth Chapel beach by road.

I love this little church for its feeling of permanence in a rapidly-changing world.

All sorts of legends exist about the enormous stone, St Levan's Stone, in the churchyard. It is precisely split in two as if by some giant cleaver and it is said to be where St Levan rested when he tired of fishing. An old prophecy states:

When with panniers astride,
A pack horse can ride
Through St Levan's Stone,
The world will be done.

St Levan's Stone, split precisely in two.

The largely fifteenth-century Church of St Levan, dedicated to Selevan, a sixth-century Celtic missionary.

Cornwall has a wealth of information and fun in its church bench ends and this one is no exception. If you look carefully you can find a jester in full traditional garb with bells; two fish on one hook, recalling the legend of St Levan; a shepherd with a crook; two eagles and a pilgrim, possibly St James.

After visiting the church, take the path across the lane, which passes beside a cottage and rises across fields, over stiles and through gateways until you come to a small Celtic cross built into a wall. Ideally you should now head due west, across a couple of fields to a green lane which leads to the hamlet of Roskestal. However, the last time we passed this way the lane was inches deep in thick mud, so we took an alternative and slightly longer route heading northwest along a well-worn footpath, across half a dozen fields and over old granite stiles, until we reached the minor road leading south to Roskestal. Follow the road roughly south-west for about a quarter of a mile, then follow it as it swings right and downhill, alongside a valleyside of bracken and heather.

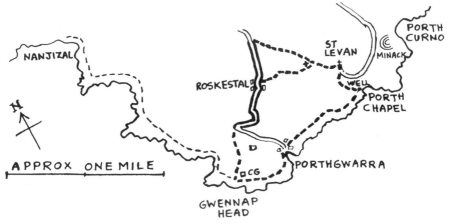

A granite farmhouse at Roskestal.

Across the valley rises the rounded mass of Gwennap Head with its coastguard station: your next goal. To reach it, take the footpath which heads down into the valley where the road turns sharp left. Cross the stream by the bridge and follow the road for a short distance before joining the path up to the headland.

This is a marvellous place for a picnic (weather permitting) with plenty to see as you relax. Apart from the coastguard lookout there are the strange black and white daymarks for shipping, the distant view of the lonely Wolf Rock lighthouse, ships passing by and a wealth of wild flowers. Particularly beautiful is the gorgeous red-brown lichen on the granite boulders forming the cliff. This lowly form of life is now thought to be the best of all monitors of pure air as it will only live and multiply where the sulphur element in the air is negligible or nil.

The small bridge below Gwennap Head.

The spectacular view from Gwennap Head looking towards Nanjizal Bay.

Our walk now carries us east, across the springy turf of the headland and down to Porthgwarra, but if you wish to lengthen your walk, head northwest to visit the only accessible beach between Gwennap Head and Land's End at Nanjizal or Mill Bay. It is another good place for a picnic or a swim in the clearest of waters. We have often seen seals here and one day we lay on a ledge and watched them literally tease a dog on the beach by coming close to the shore and suddenly appearing in the smallest offshore wave. A few years ago, after a freak storm, a sandbar formed about 150 yards below the normal low tide mark, making a perfect lagoon: deep, wide, clear and safe. Alas, the next storm restored it to normal.

Walking along this stretch of coast you may be aware of the sound of the tolling of a bell. In fact, it is the sound of the bell on the Runnel Stone buoy about a mile offshore. Rounding the headland east of Gwennap Head you descend to the tiny fishing hamlet of Porthgwarra. It is one of the very few places that has not changed since my childhood and unique in having a tunnel cut through the rocky spur dividing the two inlets. A windlass is still used for hauling the boats to safety above the high-water mark.

A path between cottages winds up onto the clifftop and leads you east along a spectacular stretch of coast back to St Levan. Before it curves inland to the church, a narrow path leads down seaward to St Levan's Holy Well with its protecting wall and then downwards to Porth Chapel beach, its crescent of sand in the lap of sheer granite walls with immense boulders at their base. Unless you are fit or have a good head for heights do not attempt to reach this beach, and if you have children with you, ensure that they are well disciplined because the path to the beach can be treacherous as well as steep.

It is here that we, as a family, have spent our happiest days: golden sand, clear water, interesting surf and completely free from all the trappings of a tourist-conscious beach. As always, the sea must be treated with respect. The wave pattern throws up powerful but short-lived waves and many people wisely stay out of it.

The Baptistry and Holy Well of St Levan, reached by fifty stone steps from the church.

Porth Chapel Cove, sheltered by high granite outcrops.

WALK TWO

Across the high eastern fringe of Bodmin Moor to the Cheesewring and Twelve Men's Moor.
MINIONS TO KILMAR TOR
OS Map (1:50,000) 201.
Length: approximately six and a half miles.

W e start this walk from the little village of Minions, near the foot of the giant television transmitter at Caradon Hill and just a couple of miles northeast of St Cleer. There is plenty of parking space in the area of the post office and the Cheesewring Hotel. The last time we did this walk we took a picnic lunch with us in our rucksack. We also took water for Tessa for it was a hot day and we laughingly say that she only does about 'six miles to the pint', which of course is an exaggeration for a dachshund until you remember that she does twice our mileage exploring and following smells.

From the southern end of the village we head northwest across the moor to look at The Hurlers, which are close by. They actually consist of three circles of stones, dating from the Bronze Age, and the same sort of legend has attached itself to them as to the Merry Maidens in West Penwith. Standing by these mysterious stones and looking north you will see Stowe's Hill and the Cheesewring over the brow of moorland. This is our next goal and a series of vague paths lead over the short sheep-cropped turf and across the cutting of an old mineral line to the famous Cheesewring Quarry.

As you reach the southern rim of the

The Hurlers: sportsmen turned to stone? Beyond is the Caradon Hill television transmitter.

The entrance to Daniel Gumb's rocky home in the shadow of the Cheesewring.

quarry you will notice a small square doorway amid a pile of rocks. This is the remains of Daniel Gumb's house – a sad tumbled heap of stones now. He was a quarry worker and a self-taught mathematician and astronomer who lived here in the 1730s with his wife and family. On the capstone is chiselled the diagram we remember from our early days of geometry to prove the theorem of Pythagoras, a right-angled triangle with a square on each of its sides. One can also see the initials 'D.G.' and the date 1735 carved on a stone by the entrance. I am told that the hut had a sliding stone door and that Gumb carved this epitaph on a gravestone at Linkinhorne church:

Here I lie by the churchyard door;
Here I lie because I'm poor.
The further in, the more you pay,
But here lie I as warm as they.

A short scramble up the side of the quarry leads you to one of Cornwall's most famous landmarks, the Cheesewring, with its large flat stones balanced

The Cheesewring perched on the very rim of the quarry.

The delicately-poised weathered rocks of the Cheesewring.

The summit of Stowe's Hill.

Across the valley from Stowe's Hill rises the granite outcrop of Sharp Tor.

precariously on smaller ones. Walking to the summit of Stowe's Hill you have marvellous views in all directions and the weathered granite here is carved into the most fantastic shapes. On a clear day you can see for miles and it is well worth the climb. But we have an even finer viewpoint as a target: the top of Cornwall's third highest point, Kilmar Tor in the far distance, slightly to the west of due north. Much nearer across the valley to the north are Langstone Downs and the jutting mass of Sharp Tor, but we will be circling this jagged peak in a clockwise direction.

Walk down the hillside from Stowe's Hill to the north until you reach a track leading to North Wardbrook Farm where, on our last visit, kindly Mr Hooper gave us some water for Tessa and told us of his life as a sheep farmer. The track which runs west from the farm was once a mineral tramway and Mr Hooper pointed out the granite setts and told us the history of the never-completed railway that headed out in the direction of Jamaica Inn.

Through the farmyard and adjacent fields with their many sheep Tessa was on her lead and when at last we released her, we insisted she stayed close to our heels. Leaving the final gateway a path leads up over Langstone Downs to Kilmar Tor, but we chose to follow the line of the railway round the base of the hill until we were due south of the Tor. After negotiating an area of boggy ground, strike off north and up to the dramatic rock formations surmounting Kilmar Tor. On the way up are countless grassy hollows suitable for a picnic. Even in a place of such high winds, we have never failed to find a sheltered spot.

Moorland sheep near North Wardbrook Farm.

The magnificent panorama from the summit of Kilmar Tor.

Kilmar Tor is part of Twelve Men's Moor, so called because the Prior of Launceston in 1284 granted a lease to twelve tin miners. (Or would they have been tin streamers, I wonder?) This is our favourite place in all our beloved Cornwall as from this lonely and little-known spot we can feast our eyes in all directions, noting the glint of water in Siblyback Lake and Colliford Lake to the right, the sea off Looe, Smallacombe Down, King Arthur's Bed and surely the most remote of all Cornish farms, Mr Lawrence's farm at Trewartha. To the north is Hawk's Tor, from the top of which my son Paul and I once watched a fox hunting below, quite oblivious of us.

South-east of Kilmar Tor is the low jagged outcrop of Bearah Tor. If you cross the moorland between the two, heading to the south of the rocks and avoiding the wide-horned shaggy cattle, you will reach an old quarry, still in use. From here a track leads down a hillside of tumbled boulders, mossy walls and lichen-covered hawthorns and oaks to the road north of the village of Henwood. By following this road through the pretty village and bearing right and then left, you will reach the hamlet of Higher Stanbear. The road now ascends slowly under the shadow of Stowe's Hill and with the triangular mass of Sharp Tor behind you, until it reaches Minions. The views east over the green valley of the River Lynher and Kit Hill beyond are truly spectacular.

We have walked this way on a frosty day in February, many times in spring and summer, and on a calm autumn afternoon. The colours of the landscape are always subtly beautiful, but do try to pick a clear day so that you can enjoy the distant views to the full.

The village of Henwood, with the engine house of Caradon Mines in the distance.

WALK THREE

A short country and riverside walk through the parish of Kea, home of the famous Kea plums.
BESIDE THE RIVER FAL TO COOMBE
OS Map (1:50,000) 204.
Length: approximately two miles.

Most Truronians will know this walk well as it has the advantage of being short enough for a winter afternoon or a summer evening. It also offers tranquillity, beauty, interest and is virtually traffic free. With the elderly, disabled or very young in mind, I can tell you that half way through this walk – at Coombe – is a spot where one can sit in a car and enjoy the peace and beauty of a creek of the River Fal.

The small beach on the banks of the Fal opposite Tolverne.

To find our starting point, leave the A39 road (Truro to Falmouth) at a point about two thirds of the distance between Truro and Playing Place, near Kea School, and drive through Porth Kea. Do not take the turning on the left to Old Kea, but continue to a point near Lower Lanner Farm where the road is fairly wide and tree lined. It is a good place to safely park your car.

Ignoring all footpaths and the road down to Coombe, take the old road heading east which climbs gently to Higher Trelease Farm where you will see a notice reading 'Unsuitable for Motors' – the understatement of the year. Looking back over a farm gate you will see excellent distant views of Truro Cathedral, Truro School and parts of Malpas. Follow the little lane along and downhill. It can be rather muddy in places so be careful to wear suitable footwear for this walk.

Almost at the river's edge, a sign points to the right, through a gate, but ignore this for a few moments and take the track on the left which winds down through dense undergrowth and over a couple of fallen trees to the river. A medieval ferry used to cross the River Fal to Tolverne here, but it has been defunct for many years. We both love the little beach here with its view across to the thatched cottage restaurant so popular with boat owners. I recall rowing there from Malpas on a wartime leave with my wife-to-be on our first outing together. Since then we have had many a good jam, cream and wasp

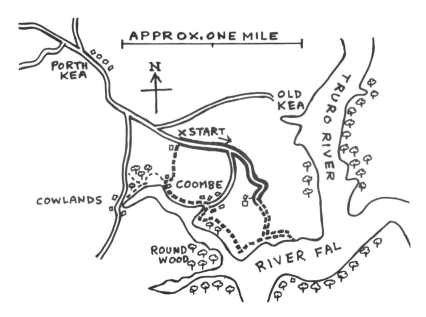

Roundwood, with its ancient quay, at the entrance to Coombe Creek.

tea there! My wife, who was living in the parish of St Michael Penkevil across the river, remembers the incident in 1940 when a Free French destroyer was bombed here, and later in the war when the river was packed with American transports and troops preparing for D-Day.

Walking back up from the stony beach, follow the signpost and join the rather wet and muddy path that takes you by fields, stiles, woods and plum orchards towards the little village of Coombe. As the path meanders along you will receive many surprise glimpses of the giant ships laid up in the deep waters of the Fal. You may also see the King Harry Ferry crossing the river and, at the opposite entrance to Coombe Creek, is the Roman quay of Roundwood, with its prehistoric British

encampment beyond on a small wooded hill. This quay marked the end, or the beginning, of a packhorse trail from the tin and copper mines as far away as Lanner and St Day. Now the property of the National Trust, it makes a lovely foreground view looking across to the nature trails of Trelissick over the brow of the hill.

The Coombe end of the path is a tunnel of overgrown entwined plum trees with dappled sunshine at your feet. Coombe itself looks just as it did when I was a child and walked here with my parents. Apples, oysters and plums dominate all the activities, and if you do this walk at the end of August or in early September you will find plums for sale outside almost every house, and delicious they are too. For many Cornish folk, a visit to Coombe at

The creekside hamlet of Coombe.

19

Low tide at Coombe Creek.

plum time is a regular date on the calendar.

Continuing along the creekside, the footpath leads up to a house which has a stall selling bric-a-brac alongside it. A track winds round the right of the house and up across fields, past Lower Lanner Farm, to the road where you parked your car. But you may wish to continue your walk as far as Cowlands at the head of the creek. At low tide you can walk along the beach, but at other times you can follow a path which leads, below a wood, to the peaceful little hamlet. A metalled lane then takes you from here up past Higher Lanner Farm and, turning right, back to your car.

Plum orchards at Cowlands.

WALK FOUR

A walk across heathland and rolling sandhills to high headlands and secluded beaches.
AROUND THE KELSEYS TO PENTIRE POINT
OS Map (1:50,000) 200.
Length: approximately four miles.

We start this walk from a field car-park literally at the end of the road leading from Crantock to West Pentire, after passing through a little hamlet with an inn, a village shop and hotel. Before heading southwards it is tempting to follow the road west, then turning right for a view over Crantock Beach and across The Gannel to the headland of Pentire Point East. But do not linger long, for we will pass this way again on our return journey.

From the car-park entrance turn left and walk southwards down a farm lane which meanders steeply to a sandy valley with a little stream flowing through it to the sea. Almost hidden there, on the other side of the stream, is a small National Trust car-park. Passing this and ignoring the foot-path to Porth Joke by the 'No Camping' sign, climb up the path heading due south, past a disused quarry, and onto Cubert Common. A little way up the valley, where the track crosses a small stream, a path

Looking north across The Gannel to Pentire Point East, the concluding stretch of the walk.

strikes off to the right, heading southwest and up over The Kelseys.

This high common of open grazing land is now owned by the National Trust and provides excellent walking. On reaching the brow of the hill, follow the line of a fence and wall on your right, then pass through a gate by a National Trust sign and turn left, following the same wall, now on your left. This area must have been well

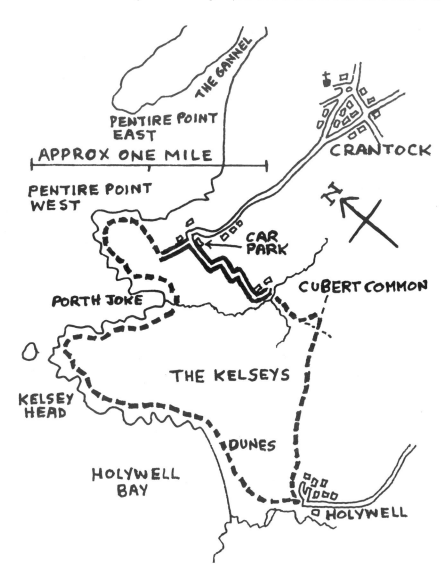

The boardwalk through the area of dunes being reclaimed.

known to John Wesley (no doubt on horseback) as he frequently stayed at Carines Farm, a mile or so to the east, while preaching locally. The short turf slowly gives way to sandy dunes as you skirt a golf course and descend into the village of Holywell, a good place to pause for refreshment.

Heading north-west towards the beach, the footpath curves off to the north, across the sand dunes. This whole area of dunes is in the process of being reclaimed, and walking is sensibly limited to a wooden boardwalk which twists, rises and falls quite wonderfully around the contours of the dunes. On reaching the coastal footpath at the northern end of the bay, you find yourself with a dramatic view over Holywell Beach with Penhale Point and Gull Rock just seawards. This is a

Holywell Beach, with its broad stretch of sand and fine surf.

good place for a picnic, with a grandstand view of the surfers showing grace and skill in often mountainous seas. From here you can also see the cave which contains what most people think of as the holy well. Many times as a child I climbed the fifteen slippery dark steps leading to a little rock well or spring, where I made a wish. I was later told that the real holy well is, in fact, about a mile inland from here near Trevornick Farm, on the way to Cubert, with its little spire looking like a poised twentieth-century missile.

The path now rises as we walk north to the tip of Kelsey Head, with the outline of an ancient cliff castle still visible at its very extremity and with the Chick Rock below. This rock has seal breeding caves on its seaward side and we have often watched seals swimming here. At very low spring tide and in calm weather conditions, the adventurous cross over with hook-ended poles to find lobsters and crabs, but it is a dangerous expedition.

From the site of the hill fort there is a very fine view looking northeast, along the dramatic coastline and beaches all the way to Trevose Head, with the white lighthouse just visible. I remember coming out here with the family in a full gale and I have a photograph of us 'leaning on the wind'. On my last visit, in calmer weather, we sat and watched a sparrowhawk swooping and hovering in the updraughts of warm air.

Now our path takes us round the headland and towards Porth Joke ('Polly Joke' to us locals) where we have spent hundreds of happy days over the last fifty years and which is just as unspoilt now as when I was a child. I have spent many an evening surfing here, after a day's work, with the sun setting into the sea as a background.

Looking back from Pentire Point West, with Porth Joke on the left.

Kelsey Head with its Chick Rock.

After crossing the beach we once again pick up the coastal footpath around West Pentire. As the path climbs, look back over the beach to The Kelseys beyond: not a building in sight! Around Pentire Point West we come to Vugga Cove; again, a favourite place for an evening swim in the gulley of deep water 500 yards beyond the surf when the tide is low, and sandy at low spring tide. Here we head inland along the track which leads us back to the car-park, past the Bowgie Inn through the gorse and heather.

Of all my favourite walks in Cornwall, this one comes among the 'top five'.

26

WALK FIVE

An all-weather walk round one of Cornwall's
most famous headlands.
KINGSAND TO RAME HEAD
OS Map (1:50,000) 201.
Length: approximately five miles.

The special attraction of this walk is that the majority of it is on tarmac, making it equally suitable for a slow summer stroll or a breezy walk on a winter's day. For this we can thank the earls of Mount Edgcumbe who began building a carriageway along the coast as far as Kingsand in the early eighteenth century, and continued it as far as Penlee Point in the early nineteenth century. In fact, almost all this entire walk is on coastal land owned by the Mount Edgcumbe Country Park.

We begin in the twin villages of Kingsand and Cawsand, two of our most unspoilt fishing villages. The latter was reputed to be one of the worst smuggling villages on the Cornish coast. Strange though it may seem, Kingsand was not a

The village of Kingsand, formerly part of Devon.

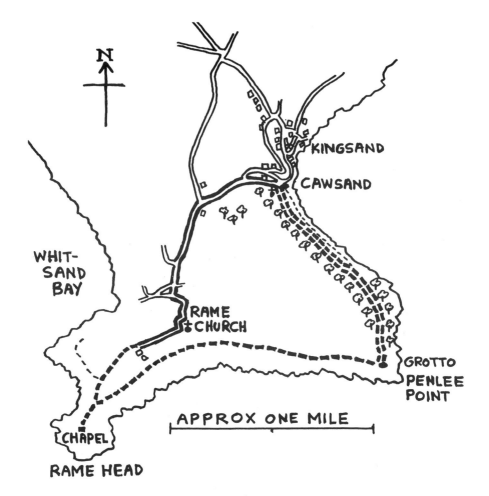

N

WHIT-
SAND
BAY

KINGSAND

CAWSAND

RAME
CHURCH

GROTTO
PENLEE
POINT

APPROX ONE MILE

CHAPEL

RAME HEAD

part of Cornwall until 1844, while neigh-bouring Cawsand was. We found a sort of proof at Boundary Cottage in Garrett Street and on the wall of the house next door where a granite marker shows the former boundary.

Having explored the steep, twisting streets of both these villages, enjoy the view out into Plymouth Sound and an 'end-on' view of the famous breakwater. I remember coming here in the late 'thirties and seeing giant transatlantic liners at anchor while their passengers travelled into Millbay Docks by tender and by fast express to London: 'Land at Plymouth and

Save a Day'. Looking to the right you can see across to the Great Mew Stone guarding the tricky entrance into the River Yealm.

To begin the walk proper, pass through Cawsand to the little square at its centre and take the lane up to the left of the church. You may find yourself on the coastal footpath, but various paths and steps lead up to the tarmac-surfaced Earl's Drive which runs straight as a die under towering trees as far as Penlee Point. This is a private road but open to pedestrians, and very beautiful it is too, with a wide variety of wonderful trees forming a high

The old boundary marker on the wall in Garrett Street.

The square in Cawsand. The path leads off to the left of the church.

The Roscoff ferry seen from the Grotto at Penlee Point.

A stile on the coastal footpath leading to Rame Head.

The little chapel dedicated to St Michael, on Rame Head.

arch above you. When the trees are in leaf, the view to your left is obscured until the track suddenly rises and emerges onto the breezy tip of Penlee Point.

Just above the brow, near the coast-guard station, is a charming grotto cut into the rock, with windows looking out over the broad mouth of the River Tamar. This unusual folly is named after Queen Adelaide, wife of William IV. We now walk west along the clearly-defined coastal footpath, bordered by a very rich variety of wild flowers. It is well worth carrying a field guide to help you identify some of the more unusual species.

Ahead of you lies the high rounded mass of Rame Head with its little ancient chapel on the top dedicated to St Michael, the patron saint of high places and sailors. It dates from the fourteenth century and legend says that hermits kept a light

Looking from a window of the chapel back to Penlee Point.

burning here as a primitive forerunner of the lighthouse. From this vantage point 300 feet above the sea you can see as far as the Lizard Peninsula on a clear day, and the Eddystone Lighthouse can just be seen ten miles off shore. To the west is the gentle sweep of Whitsand Bay. On my last visit, I tried to picture the scene here in July 1815 when H.M.S. *Belerophon* anchored below with Napoleon on board as prisoner.

Having descended from Rame Head, walk up to the car-park, just to the left of the coastguard station. From here you can just see the top of the spire of Rame Church peeping over the brow of the hill, and a narrow lane leads you to the slate Church of St Germanus with its unusual broached spire. Parts of this church date from 1259 and there are some interesting bench ends and a wagon roof. It bears a slight resemblance to the delightful church at St Enodoc, and like that building, it has no electricity, services being held by candlelight.

From the church a narrow lane winds through lovely countryside to the little hamlet of Forder, and taking the right fork here, it continues down the valley and back to Cawsand.

If you still have any energy in reserve on your return to the twin villages, a delightful series of paths straggle along the coast to the north-east. They are known as Mina-dew Breaks and to the left the land rises to a height of over 400 feet. You may just be able to see the towering walls of the now disused Grenville Battery.

We always enjoy a day in this lovely part of Cornwall, so far away from our home.

Cawsand's rooftops and tiny beach.

WALK SIX

The first stage of a marathon walk from coast to coast across Cornwall, following in the footsteps of the saints.
THE SAINTS' WAY: PADSTOW TO WITHIEL
OS Map (1:50,000) 200.
Length: approximately ten miles.

Almost thirty miles of footpaths, bridle paths, sunken lanes and minor roads lie ahead of us as we start our traverse of Cornwall from Padstow to Fowey. The 'Saints' Way' was originally a Bronze Age and Iron Age trading route across the peninsula, avoiding the often treacherous passage around Land's End and serving the trade between Ireland, Wales, Cornwall and Brittany. In the Dark Ages the route was used by Celtic Christian missionaries who crossed from Wales and Ireland, converting the Cornish and giving their names to holy wells, churches and wayside granite crosses.

The route was reopened in 1986 as a result of a C.R.S. Community Programme sponsored by the Manpower Services Commission. Eight young people spent a year hacking through brambles and nettles, building steps and stiles, constructing bridges and erecting waymarks to guide walkers. A single route leads you from Padstow, via Little Petherick, Withiel and Lanivet to Helman Tor, from where you have a choice of routes leading to Fowey: either via Luxulyan and Tywardreath or via Lanlivery and Golant. Both these final legs of the walk are splendid but, forced to make a choice, I have decided to describe the latter lesser-known route.

No-one, I imagine, would want to tackle this marathon journey in one go, so I have divided the walk into four stages, but as some of these are still rather lengthy, you may wish to sub-divide them even further.

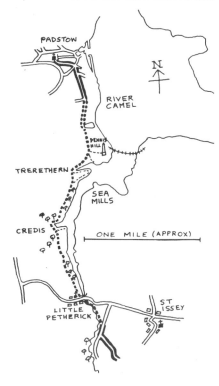

34

Padstow: the arrival point for many Irish and Welsh missionaries, and the departure point for numerous emigrating miners.

The first leg – from Padstow to Withiel – is roughly ten miles long, so you may prefer to break it at Little Petherick.

I think Desirée and I, with our dog Tessa, were among the first few of many thousands of people to savour this long-distance walk. I was very conscious of a sense of history, and that I followed in the footsteps of traders, mariners and saints. The greatest (but not Cornwall's patron saint) was St Petroc. He settled near the Camel Estuary in the sixth century, making two pilgrimages to Rome and living for thirty years at Lanwethinoc. There are numerous legends about him and his miracles, one of which was to turn water into nectar. His relics were stolen in 1177 by Augustinian monks and taken to Brittany, and this caused an international incident. The relics were finally formally returned via Dartmouth where they were 'rested' in a little chapel before being returned to Cornwall. The relics no longer exist, but the thirteenth-century ivory casket that contained them can be found in the south wall of Bodmin parish church.

And so to begin our walk. After looking round the harbour and peaceful streets of Padstow, make your way up Duke Street and Church Street to the Church of St Petroc in its wooded churchyard. This slate-built, fifteenth-century church contains a font made from blue slate from the cliffs near Harlyn Bay and some fine carved bench ends in the chancel, one of which depicts a fox preaching to geese. Near the font we found the eight-holed stocks, last used in 1840 when three drunken men fell asleep during Divine Service.

Passing through the lych-gate to the south of the church, follow a wooded path

35

The Church of St Petroc, Padstow, built of local slate.

The obelisk on Dennis Hill commemorating the Golden Jubilee of Queen Victoria in 1887.

up to Hill Street. On reaching New Street crossroads, go straight across into Dennis Road, following this and Dennis Lane down to the bottom of the valley and Dennis Creek. Following the public footpath sign, our journey now continues steeply uphill along the edge of a field to the summit of Dennis Hill. A short detour leads you through iron gates to the obelisk commemorating the Golden Jubilee of Queen Victoria in 1887. This is a good place to regain your breath and take in the points of interest. Look back at Padstow with Stepper Point beyond, and Pentire Point marking the far side of the Camel, with St Enodoc and St Mabyn parishes and Rock. Looking east, in the far distance, is the well-known shape of Rough Tor, and looking south-east you can see¯ the highest point of our walk, St Breock Downs, with St Issey Church nestling at their foot.

From this point, the walk can become rather muddy, especially after rain, and it is advisable to wear stout footwear for the majority of all four stages of the Saints' Way. Sometimes you will find it necessary to walk through mud, and when passing through farmyards, something even worse!

Our path leads us down along the borders of Little Petherick Creek, with two smaller creeks leading off it. Descending to Trerethern Creek we can see the former tidal mill, Sea Mills, on the opposite bank. Taking a short cut across the top of a field, we now follow the path above the line of scrub and gorse to Credis Creek. The large Victorian farmhouse inland is Treravel, where St Petroc is said to have died while walking to Padstow. A flight of steps leads us down the slippery hillside to Credis Creek.

Inland from here is Trevisker Farm. In 1813 a twenty-year-old St Merryn girl was hanged at Bodmin Gaol for 'setting fire to a mow of wheat at Trevisker' at the time of the corn scarcity and the subsequent miners' revolt. As we traversed this little creek by a footbridge below Credis Farm, I wondered about the days when it was used for the export of copper (and a little silver) from a mine employing fifty men in a thirty-fathom shaft. Nature has obscured all traces now.

Having crossed the creek, do not take the path along the bankside, but head up to the south across fields. Follow the public footpath signs across some slate stiles. The path slowly descends through a little copse where you can find snow-drops, primroses and bluebells in season, with the sound of curlews always in your ears.

Little Petherick Creek with Sea Mills on the far bank and St Breock Downs on the horizon.

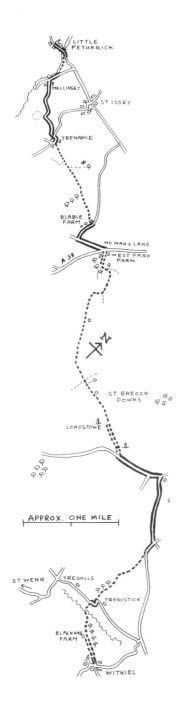

Little Petherick's Church of St Petroc, built into the hillside.

A short track leads to Little Petherick and the A389. The church, again dedicated to St Petroc, hugs the hillside and is one of the most unusual on this walk. It was restored by Athelston Riley who employed Sir Ninian Comper to carry out the work in 1898. The glass is richly coloured; there is a fine painted screen and Mrs Riley is immortalised in bronze in a small chapel. Athelstan Riley himself designed the tiny village hall beside the bridge in 1907.

Suddenly, for the first time since leaving Padstow, we can hear traffic on the busy A389, and it makes an unpleasant change from the relative peace of the walk so far. Crossing the bridge we walk a short distance up the main road: a complete contrast to the peace of the high uplands ahead of us. A blue-slate stile leads us down across a field and along the valley to Mellingey with its attractive cottages and mill house. A quiet minor road then leads us to the small hamlet of Trenance. Here we turn east along a track and down into a valley, passing a slate quarry.

After crossing the stream by two footbridges and following the path across

39

The blue-slate stile near Little Petherick leading down to the valley and the hamlet of Mellingey.

a couple of fields we reach Blable Farm. Leaving the farmyard, turn right along the lane, then left until you reach the busy A39, which is a stretch of road familiar to visitors to the Royal Cornwall Show at Whitecross, a mile and a half to the north-east. Cross the road to West Park Farm and No Man's Land and follow a rather muddy track for a few hundred yards. Taking the path to the left, follow it up the wooded hill, bearing to the right until you reach a series of fields and specially-built stiles.

So begins the gradual ascent of St Breock Downs, hitherto unknown to me, so a particular joy. We walked this section through eight or nine large fields against the continuous background music of multitudes of skylarks, occasional pheasant 'squacks' and the multitone bleats of hundreds of sheep. A couple of buzzards wheeled overhead. The view to the north, over the showground site and the town of Wadebridge, is quite remarkable. A rabbit started up under our feet and Tessa, our dog, signalled her acceleration with a hunting cry that was all in vain.

Shortly after passing the little farm of Pawtonsprings, surely one of Cornwall's

most lonely and isolated, we were standing at 700 feet above sea level with the skyline dominated by large burial barrows and a huge standing stone, the Long-stone. This sixteen-foot-high stone is a religious monument of the Bronze Age (1800–600 BC) and was once surrounded by a cairn. It became a medieval meeting place, hence its name, *Mene Gurta*, Stone of Waiting. Looking north-west we could trace the way we had walked, with the Camel Estuary dominating the view, and the tower of St Issey Church already a long way behind us. To the north-east we looked down on Wadebridge with St Mabyn a little beyond, with the woods sheltering Pencarrow and the two great mounds of Rough Tor and Brown Willy as a gigantic backcloth to the whole scene.

The Stone of Waiting, a Bronze Age monument.

The isolated farm at Pawtonsprings.

If we thought we had seen sheep in abundance we were now seeing an even higher density with a multitude of young lambs. Their antics were a joy to behold. On reaching the road turn left and then take the second turning on the right, near St Breock Downs Farm. Now at last you are actually travelling downhill and looking directly into Hustyn Wood and some of the least-known and most beautiful parts of inland Cornwall. We often strayed from the Saints' Way to enjoy the tranquillity of some nearby places. Ruthern Bridge, Grogley, Burlawn and Polbrook Bridge are a 'must', and we enjoyed the tranquillity of St Breock with its steep-sided stream, a tributary of the Camel, flowing through it. We wondered how such a large medieval church could be so hidden until you come right upon it.

Back to the walk. Having passed the entrance to Hustyn's Health Hydro the road turns south. After a short distance we leave the road and set off due south along a track and across the eastern edge of two fields. Crossing the next large field diagonally we reach the head of an ancient stony track leading beneath trees down to Tregustick Farm. Our goal for this section of the walk, Withiel Church, is visible across the valley, and to the south-east can be seen the granite outcrop of Helman Tor, a later goal, and Bodmin Beacon with its obelisk.

At Tregustick Farm follow the road down to the ford. The stream is in fact quite deep here and we were thankful for the two wooden bridges which enabled us to continue without having to take a paddle. After trudging up the steep hillside, you reach the charming village of Withiel with its church dedicated to St Clement. It has an oak-ribbed roof and painted slate commandment boards.

So we come to the end of the first – and longest – stage of the Saints' Way walk.

Withiel Church, top left, lies across the valley with Tregustick and Blackhay Farms below.

WALK SEVEN

The second stage of the Saints' Way, across rolling countryside, past ancient Celtic crosses, to a high, granite vantage point.

THE SAINTS' WAY: WITHIEL TO HELMAN TOR
OS Map (1:50,000) 200.
Length: approximately seven miles.

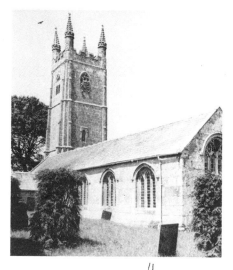

Having walked through the parishes of Padstow, Little Petherick, St Issey and St Breock, we now approach the half-way point on the Saints' Way and continue to one of its highest points, Helman Tor.

Before we start, the village of Withiel, set amid pleasant rolling countryside, is worth exploring. Alongside the medieval Church of St Clement is a delightful rectory, and the straggle of cottages and colourful gardens have a peaceful quality about them. We have found this village a good starting point for a little-known walk to such lovely places as Demelza, Langew and St Wenn.

Withiel's medieval Church of St Clement.

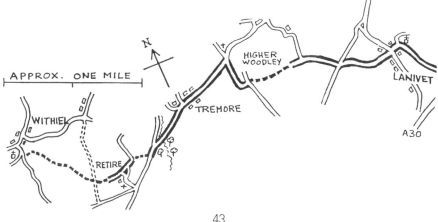

43

The cottage post office in Withiel.

Back to the Saints' Way, we take the road south to a twelve per cent gradient sign on the left where a stile leads into a farmyard and past a ripe-smelling silage heap. Over another stile and diagonally across two fields, the path dips to a valley bottom and a fine granite stile over a stream. It was somewhere near here that the original settlement of Withiel was founded by a Celtic saint named Zota. Cross the next two fields diagonally, heading south-west, until you come to stiles leading into and out of a narrow, flowery green lane. From here it is a short walk to the hamlet of Retire.

A clapper bridge at Tremorebridge. It is without parapets to cope easily with flood water.

On this section of the walk we had one of our grandsons, Simon, with us and as we approached Retire Farm with Tessa on a lead (the field contained sheep and lambs), we were amazed to see two lambs bounding and leaping towards us. Tessa, especially, was nonplussed by the extraordinary behaviour from what were most obviously hand-reared and human-loving lambs. Incidentally, I am informed that the name Retire has nothing to do with the tranquil atmosphere, but comes from the old Cornish *red hyr*, long ford.

On reaching Retire, walk straight across the top of the hamlet and along a track. Cross a stile on the right and cross the field to a gate in the far corner. Closing the gate behind you, you will see, immediately on your right, a stile and some very steep steps leading down to the road. For a mile or so, mostly uphill, we now follow the minor road over the double clapper bridges at Tremorebridge with their little streams running down to join the Camel at Ruthernbridge. Houses with miniature triangular windows face each other here.

After passing Tremore Farm and eighteenth-century Manor (now, appro-priately for the Saints' Way, a Christian

The familiar Forth an Syns–Saints' Way *marker you will find on stiles, gates and posts along the route.*

Fellowship Centre) we reach a high point at a crossroads where stands an ancient cross. We also find the now familiar yellow *Forth an Syns*–Saints' Way marker pointing south to a spot near Higher Woodley where a footpath continues

45

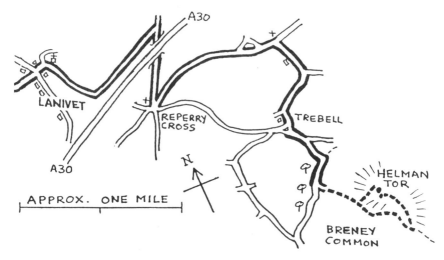

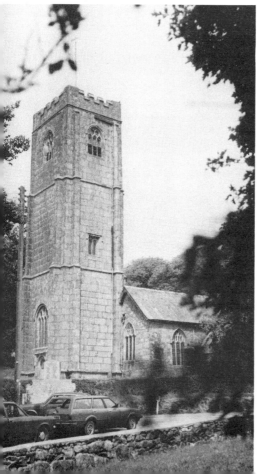

Lanivet's parish church.

across fields for half a mile. Minor roads lead us gently downhill, across the old coach road from Mount Pleasant to Bodmin, to the lovely self-contained village of Lanivet, where the busy A389 is such a contrast.

This is the half-way point of our marathon walk and a good place to follow the example of our ancestors who walked this way and stop for some welcome refreshment. Away from the main road is the delightful triangular village green and the parish church, dedicated to St Nivet, beside a fast-running stream. Within its walls are a fifteenth-century font and the remains of a Saxon column. Henderson's *Church Guide* says that a document exists to show that in 1539 the parishioners of Lanivet purchased four of the bells of the dissolved Bodmin priory for £36; so Bodmin's loss was Lanivet's gain.

After inspecting the ancient crosses in the churchyard, the tenth-century graves by the south porch and the fine yew trees, we now continue our journey by following Rectory Road due south. At the top of Rectory Hill the road makes a detour eastwards to a tunnel under the A30. This stretch of the Bodmin bypass may not be marked on some older O.S. maps. The sleek concrete curves of this stretch of road are a great contrast to the winding ways and green lanes we have seen so far.

At Reperry Cross is a delightful guide stone on which a hand points the way, as well as the cross itself. I am told that the word Reperry comes from the old Cornish words for Petroc's ford. Turn left at the crossroads and continue for about a mile to St Ingunger and another wayside Celtic

One of several inscribed Celtic crosses in the churchyard at Lanivet.

cross. Follow the Saints' Way marker due south to the hamlet of Fentonpits and yet another cross. At the fork in the road, turn south-west to Trebell and then south-east to Trebell Green with its fine stone hedge-banks. The road soon turns sharply to the right and we come to Helman Tor Gate. The second highest point of our walk, Helman Tor at 680 feet, is beyond.

A guiding hand along the way at Reperry Cross. The mason obviously underestimated the length of the word 'Lanivet'.

The granite outcrop of Helman Tor, one of the finest vantage points in Cornwall.

Close inspection of the marker on the gate will show not two directions marked, but three, for this is the point at which the path divides, like the two prongs of a tuning fork. The remainder of our journey to Fowey can be taken along a choice of two routes: via Luxulyan and St Blazey or via Lanlivery and Golant. We will be taking the second of these routes; so to bring this section of the walk to a conclusion, we will tackle the exhilarating climb to the summit of Helman Tor.

The view from the rocky top is truly magnificent. We are now surrounded by acres of willow, broom and gorse, with Breney Common below to the west. The obelisk memorial to Sir Walter Raleigh Gilbert lies to the north, overlooking Bodmin. On another side the dark mass of Roche Rock and the irregular man-made mountains of china-clay spoil dominate the landscape. In fact, it seems that all mid Cornwall is available for inspection below us.

Just below the summit outcrop a large logan rock is poised. You have to experiment to get the 'rocking angle' just right, but to feel this massive granite boulder, weighing at least ten tons, moving beneath you is a remarkable experience. On our last visit we all climbed on it – grandparents, children, grandchildren and dogs – and rocked and rocked as Cornish people must have done for centuries.

A walker tries out the logan rock near the summit.

WALK EIGHT

The third stage of the Saints' Way: down from the rocky heights to deep wooded valleys.
THE SAINTS' WAY: HELMAN TOR TO LANLIVERY AND MILLTOWN
OS Map (1:50,000) 200.
Length: approximately four and a half miles.

From either Helman Tor Gate or the summit of Helman Tor itself, head south-east along the track which runs between Breney Common and the western flank of the Tor. After passing a small car-park continue along the walled track and ignore the public footpath sign pointing west. The views looking back up to the

rocky heights and ahead over the countryside are splendid. This ancient hedged track, which was almost certainly a prehistoric trading route between the two coasts, slopes gently down until you reach a minor road.

Head south-east to a crossroads where stands a disused Bible Christian chapel

The summit of Helman Tor.

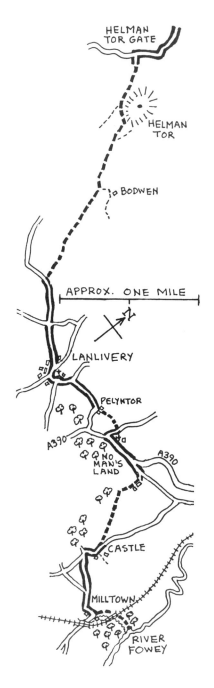

before climbing to the hilltop village of Lanlivery with its pinnacled fifteenth-century church tower, Cornwall's second tallest after Probus. The church is dedicated to St Brevita, but its Feast Day is on St Dunstan's Day (19 May) so you can take your pick! One side of the tower used to be painted white as a landmark for sailors off Gribbin Head six miles south, but presumably only before the great daymark was built there in 1842.

In the tower is a painted board of rhymes for bellringers: five little men in odd hats ringing five bells, so it must have been painted before 1811 when the number of bells was increased to eight. The rhyme begins:

Hark how the chirping Treble sings
most clear,
And covering Tom comes rolling in the
rear;
Now throw them up on end that all
may see
What laws are best to keep sobriety;
We ring the quick to church the dead to
grave ...

Churchtown Farm Field Studies Centre at Lanlivery, with the second highest church tower in Cornwall beyond.

We move from ancient history to a remarkable bit of modern history by just crossing the road from church to farm. Here is the Churchtown Farm Field Studies Centre which provides the great Cornish act of compassion of the giving of holidays to handicapped children. The farmyard is filled with specially adapted coaches, hydraulic lifts for wheelchairs, canoes and all the equipment needed for our less fortunate friends to have the holiday of a lifetime. My wife and I have met groups of them in remote parts of Bodmin Moor and on the river at Lerryn and hold the whole imaginative project in very high esteem. Long may it be well supported by money and people with vocation.

Having enjoyed an excellent bar lunch at the Old Crown Inn opposite the church, we admired the pretty cottage gardens and gothic-style schoolhouse. We then took the gate at the eastern side of the churchyard and descended the stone steps, passing a well-restored Meeting House. Following the lane eastwards towards Lostwithiel you pass the mysteriously-named Powderham Castle Caravan Park and arrive at a cottage, Pelyntor, where the road bends south. Go through the private-looking gate here, between the buildings, and through what seems to be a sheep pen before crossing a stile into two fields.

Over the rise the footpath descends to a point near the junction of the B3269 and A390 where a twelve-foot high Celtic cross stands on a grass island. We now head east along the busy main road towards Lostwithiel for a short stretch before coming to the granite gateposts of Pelyn on the right. Go along the lane passing the gateposts and right again, up the hill to the farm, taking the green lane south.

East of the churchyard are a restored Meeting House and some charming cottages.

The Celtic cross beside the A390.

From the fields above Castle you look over the Fowey Valley and the rolling fields of St Sampson parish.

Unfortunately on our last visit this farm track became a nightmare of mud and slurry for nearly a quarter of a mile and my wife, Tessa our dog and myself were quite disgustingly filthy by the time we descended through the trees and joined the minor road at Castle. The view from this track over the lush countryside is magnificent, but if you wish to avoid the mud, keep straight on when reaching Pelyn's gateposts, walking downhill to Lostwithiel cemetery before turning south to Castle.

From Castle take the minor road south. Just before a junction where we turned left along a lovely wooded valley, we found a stream and were thankfully able to wash off the mud from ourselves and give Tessa an ad hoc bath! Following the lane down the valley we reached Milltown: no smoking factory chimneys but a peaceful little hamlet of charming cottages.

The Saints' Way route here takes the road south, but first we decided to follow the footpath east through the dense woods, past the old mill house and over a wooden bridge, to the banks of the River Fowey. Looming over our heads, almost hidden by the trees, was the mighty viaduct carrying the main railway line to London. We must have passed over it at speed many times without ever suspecting what a peaceful little valley lay beneath.

A short stroll led through the woods to the mineral line alongside the mudflats of the River Fowey. As we watched the wading birds on the far bank, a train, the *Tre Pol Pen*, rattled past pulling forty-four wagons of china clay to Fowey for export. We then retraced our steps through the wood to the hamlet of Milltown, and the final leg of this journey across Cornwall.

The upper tidal reaches of the River Fowey near Milltown.

Roses round the door at Milltown.

WALK NINE

The final stage of a journey along ancient riverside tracks and footpaths, through Tristan and Iseult country.
THE SAINTS' WAY: MILLTOWN TO GOLANT AND FOWEY
OS Map (1:50,000) 200.
Length: approximately five and a half miles.

So we begin the final stage of our journey from Padstow to Fowey, across the waist of Cornwall. From Milltown, less than a mile from the centre of Lostwithiel, head south, under the railway bridge. We come to a narrow tarmac lane on the left which climbs slowly to the top of a rounded ridge. As we set off along this two-mile meandering lane, the farm below is Lantyan, an ancient building said to have been built on the site of the palace of King Mark, uncle of Tristan and husband of Iseult.

Gates in the high hedges on either side afford superb views over rolling farmland to the west and across the river valley to the east with its riverbank Church of St Winnow. The lane is soon bordered on the left by Lantyan and Woodgate woods. Descending to the foot of the valley,

Fine views of rolling countryside from the lane near Milltown.

ignore the turning to Wringford Farm and cross the stream before climbing the far valleyside.

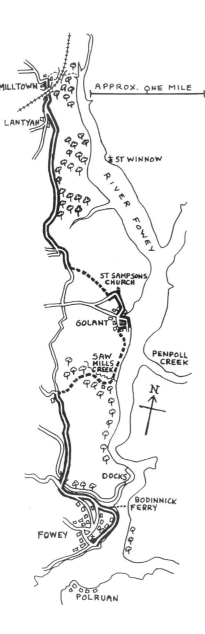

After a short distance you will see the familiar *Foth an Syns*–Saints' Way sign near a gate on the left, directing you over a stile into a field. After so much lane walking, I was pleased to feel grass under my feet again. After a couple of fields and stiles, cross a drive and continue diagonally across a large field to a wooden gate. Pause here and look north-west. In the distance you can clearly see the pinnacles of Lanlivery Church with Helman Tor beyond. Across the valley to the west is Castle Dore, the site of the military headquarters of King Mark.

Passing through the gate we now descend slowly, crossing a stile in the hedge, until we reach a lane leading to St Sampson Church and Golant. We once found this path across the fields 'protected' by two horses that seemed very anxious to prevent us continuing by simulated galloping attacks. We were quite glad to reach the safety of the stile! Turn left at the lane and before you stands the Parish Church of St Sampson, with the tower of St Veep Church on the hilltop across the river.

The Church of St Sampson, where King Mark and Queen Iseult worshipped.

The peaceful interior of the church with its old barrel roof.

The riverside village of Golant, popular with the boating fraternity.

Lovers of the Tristan and Iseult romance will be at home here, for St Sampson Church is where King Mark and Queen Iseult worshipped. West of Fowey (you may pass it on your way home) is the Tristan Stone. Dating from the sixth century, it is inscribed *'DRUSTANUS HIC IACIT CUNOMORI FILIUS'* or 'Here lies Drustan (Tristan), son of Cunomorus (Mark)'. The interior of this charming church is spanned by a barrel roof with carved oak beams, and outside, alongside the porch, is St Sampson's Holy Well.

Leaving the church by the little gate beneath an ancient oak tree, we walk steeply down to the riverside village of Golant. It was here that Charles Stuart camped overnight before the surrender of the Parliamentarian army in 1644, and 200 years later where Garibaldi came to stay with Colonel Peard. We were aware of the distant smell of marine paint, and at least a dozen boats of all sizes were being worked on in preparation for the season. The road near the bottom of the village has a sign warning that unattended vehicles might be flooded at high tide.

A rumble that grew louder and louder resolved itself into a train hauling thirty wagons of china clay along the riverside to Fowey. We enjoyed the hospitality of the Fishermen's Arms and a visit to the Post Office Stores, a delightful little shop where Mrs Rundle seems to stock everything.

We set off for the last couple of miles to Fowey along a footpath leading from a short, steep hill out of Golant and behind the Cormorant Hotel. The next mile of high, hillside footpath proved to be, in our minds, the most beautiful in all the twenty-six miles since we left Padstow. In spring the hillside is bright with millions of primroses; in summer the bracken grows high and in autumn the blackberries are plentiful. On our last visit, the River Fowey down below was at low tide and an unusually large sandbank was showing. From a superbly sited seat we watched people and dogs as they walked about below on these dry areas. A lot of digging for bait was going on, and some maintenance of boats, high and dry for a few hours. Opposite was Penpoll Creek, twisting away inland, and upriver was the wooded entrance to the creek that once we walked until we reached the lovely village of Lerryn. (See Book One.)

Low tide on the River Fowey, with Penpoll Creek winding away to the east.

57

The Bodinnick car ferry in mid-river.

The path eventually leads down steps to what locals call Sawmills Creek, with a stream, a little waterfall and acres of wild garlic in spring. We realized that all the material for the building of the mill must have been brought to the site by boat, as behind there is a steep wooded hillside (a mass of bluebells in spring) through which the path leads up and up. After crossing a couple of fields we reach a narrow tarmac lane, actually a continuation of the one we left earlier. And so downhill, past Penventinue Farm and over a bridge, across the English China Clay's road, along which heavily-laden lorries follow the course of the old mineral line from Par to Fowey docks.

Reaching the main road into the town, it is a short walk to Bodinnick Ferry, that ancient crossing point dating back to 1344. As we stood at the foot of the slipway, we realized that our journey from coast to coast was at an end – well, not quite! Having started our marathon walk at St Petroc's Church in Padstow, our walk would terminate at the fine parish church dedicated to St Fimbarros. It is a wonderful building with a 126-foot-tall tower, built in the fifteenth century, and with traceried battlements and four pinnacles with a weather-vane on each. Above stands the Tudor house simply called Place, the seat of the Treffry family, which was largely rebuilt in the 1840s.

The view upriver from Town Quay.

59

We marked the end of our long walk by sitting with a welcome bar meal in the Fowey Hotel. Below we noticed a strange orange craft specially designed to carry handicapped young people in their wheelchairs. It was heading out to sea. Earlier on this walk we had passed the Lanlivery Churchtown Farm Field Studies Centre, and this was one example of its marvellous work. We strained our eyes to see the name of the craft; it was *Spirit of Cornwall*.

Journey's end: the Church of St Fimbarros, Fowey.

WALK TEN

Along spectacular clifftops and across prehistoric fields,
stopping to look at curious church epitaphs.
ZENNOR TO RIVER COVE
OS Map (1:50,000) 203.
Length: approximately five miles.

Although this walk is on the shortish side, it can be rather strenuous at times and the path throughout the coastal section is very rocky, so I would strongly advise wearing some strong-soled footwear. Lest this warning put you off, I would quickly add that it is one of the most exhilarating, spectacular and atmos-

pheric walks in Cornwall, and worth any amount of wear on your feet.

The tiny village of Zennor, west of St Ives, can be reached by the coastal road which dips and twists between the high moorland and prehistoric fields which slope down to the coast. It is one of the most unspoilt areas of Britain, and long

The Wayside Cottage Folk Museum and the Church of St Senara.

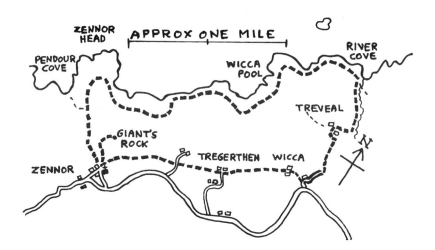

may it remain so. You can leave your car just downhill from the church and the old inn, The Tinners' Arms.

One cannot think of Zennor without thinking of the legend of the Mermaid and Matthew Trewhella, and on the bench ends in the church, carved 500 years ago, we found her with a mirror in one hand and a comb in the other. If, when you visit the church, you find one of the seats is damp, you will know you have just missed her! The outside of the church provides a lot of interest to people who are fascinated by the history that can be found on tombstones and their epitaphs. I have spent many hours recording them and wondering about their associations. On the outside wall of Zennor Church, near the gated entrance, you will find a memorial to John Davey, who, it is said, was speaking colloquial Cornish in 1891. ('Dolly' Pentreath, who died in 1777, is often regarded as the last person to speak Cornish as her first language.) Moffat's translation of the Book of Proverbs is quoted on John Davey's memorial: 'The words of a wise man are as a deep pool, a flowing stream, a fountain of life.'

Look further and you will find another quaint epitaph which has a strange ring in the world of sex equality:

Hope, fear, false joy and trouble
Are these four winds which daily toss
   this bubble.
His breath's a vapour and his life's a
   span;
'Tis glorious misery to be born a man!

Then there is the sundial that Paul Quick presented in 1737 as a thanksgiving. One of his family, 'Henny' Quick, was a poet of Zennor who died in 1857. He wrote of his parents:

My father laboured underground
Mother the spinning wheel put around.

We found another of these old epitaphs at Old Kea, near Truro:

Pray cast an eye, all that pass by,
As you are now, so once was I.
As I am now, soon you will be.
Therefore prepare to follow me.

To which some wit has added:

To follow you I've no intent.
I do not know which way you went!

62

Zennor's legendary mermaid.

The charming Cornish kitchen in the folk museum.

Before leaving the village, do call in at the charming Wayside Cottage Folk Museum, with its traditional Cornish kitchen and remarkable collection of domestic tools, quarrying and mining implements. Mr Williamson has added a splendid water wheel which stands near the entrance.

Walking north along the rocky track you will soon reach Zennor Head, 350 feet above the sea and affording one of Cornwall's finest views. The gorse, heather and thyme combine with the blue of the sea to make a breathtaking sight. Taking the path eastwards you will find yourself climbing up and scrambling down

The magnificent view from the top of Zennor Head.

This granite stile is on the clifftop path to Wicca Pool.

'like a fiddler's elbow'. The temptation is to walk and enjoy the views, but seldom is it wise or safe to do so.

Rounding Tregerthen Cliff you will then find yourself looking down into Wicca Pool and a dramatic cleft known as Cornelias Zawn. Eventually you will reach a lawn-like grassy clifftop with a little beach below. The rocks beyond contain seal caves and on one visit we counted six seals bobbing about inquisitively. A year or two ago, on a still, hot summer's day at low tide, we swam in a gulley between the rocks, quite close to some seals. They neither moved away nor came closer and so we observed the same courtesy.

On reaching River Cove you will discover two paths ahead of you. Take the one on the right which climbs inland, up the side of a charming sheltered valley. The undergrowth becomes denser and the wild flowers more varied as you follow

A dark sea pounds the rocky cliffs at Wicca Pool.

65

D.H. Lawrence lived for nearly two years at Tregerthen. On the moorland beyond stands Eagle's Nest and the Poorhouse.

the stream uphill. We once saw an adder coiled on a rock by the path in this valley. When you reach a track, turn right past some cottages, and when you reach a house on your left, turn left and follow the track inland.

When you reach Boscubben Farm, just before the main road, take the track on the right which leads to the farm at Wicca. Passing through the farmyard the footpath now returns to Zennor across stiles and fields in an almost straight line, roughly following the line of some overhead cables. Gridded stones in gaps in the hedges, known as Cornish stiles, lead to the hamlet of Tregerthen. It was near here that D.H. Lawrence, his German-born wife Frieda, and Katherine Mansfield lived for a short time during the First World War. Lawrence and his wife had a pretty miserable time as the local people were convinced that they were German spies. Towering on the rocks to the south are

two houses: Eagle's Nest and the old parish Poorhouse of Zennor.

As you continue west across the fields, over stiles which must have been well known to D.H. Lawrence on his way to The Tinners' Arms, you will notice that the fields are small and irregularly shaped. Many date from the Iron Age, and this whole area is rich in prehistoric settlements. A detailed map in the Wayside Museum shows their whereabouts.

After passing south of Tremedda Farm you will soon see the tower of Zennor Church just visible over the hedges, and on reaching the village it is worth a short detour to visit the Giant's Rock just to the north. It has a capstone six yards long standing over seven stones.

This is a splendid walk at any time of the year (though sections could be rather muddy after heavy rain), and this route offers a wide variety of scenery at every stage and is highly recommended.

The mighty Giant's Rock.

WALK ELEVEN

A riverside walk, past quiet creeks,
to the village of Flushing.
PENRYN TO TREFUSIS POINT
OS Map (1:50,000) 204.
Length: approximately five miles.

This is a walk of interest whatever the season: even in the leafless depths of winter there is plenty to see. As the starting point of the walk is Penryn and the finishing point Flushing, the best idea is to use Falmouth as a base, travelling to Penryn by bus and returning by ferry. But before you catch the bus on the Moor, check that the ferry is operating; it does not run on a Sunday during the winter months.

Take the bus to Penryn and walk along the main street, past the town hall, and down one of the steep streets to Church Road. Make your way up Church Hill to St Gluvias Church and here you will be greeted by a notice affixed to the door reading:

> Every time I pass a church,
> I pay a little visit.
> So when at last I'm carried in,
> The Lord won't say 'Who is it?'

St Gluvias was Welsh, a nephew of St Petroc, and he settled by the Penryn River in the sixth century, gathering converts. The church was built in the fifteenth century and largely rebuilt by J.P. St Aubyn in 1883. It was providential that a parachute land mine which landed thirty yards from the church in 1941 did not explode,

St Gluvias Church in Penryn.

68

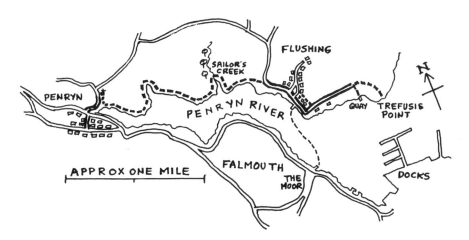

The start of the walk by the Penryn River.

whereas the church institute was destroyed by another bomb in the same year. In the churchyard is a memorial to Stephen Phillips who died in 1745 aged thirty-three and which bears a rather gruesome carving of a skull and crossbones.

From below the churchyard we took the little footpath which runs alongside the Penryn River, at the foot of small fields and past an odd assortment of rotting hulks, smart cruisers, rusting catamarans and dapper dinghies. Here and there are small paths down to the shingle river

One of the many interesting craft in Sailors' Creek.

beaches and there are pleasant views back to the town of Penryn, rising on its hill, and across the river to Ponsharden.

The path winds round the edge of a creek and through reed beds, then over a stile and past the slipway below Pencreek House. Soon you reach Sailors' Creek where a fascinating collection of craft lines the banks, all seemingly being repaired, reconstructed or reconditioned. You can also look down on the ribs of several wrecks jutting from the mud at low tide. Passing oyster beds, and with rabbits scuttling over the tree roots alongside the path, continue until you reach Falmouth Boat Construction yard where the path joins the metalled road into Flushing. The Royal Standard Inn offered us real home-made pasties or scallops *au gratin* and we had the best of both worlds by eating the scallops and taking the pasties to deal with later at Trefusis Point.

Flushing is quite unchanged since I knew it as a boy because it is off any 'throughways'. Its Celtic name was Nankersey and today there is a famous choir of that name. It is said that the architecture of its houses (so like Topsham in Devon) was influenced by Dutch engineers who lived here while helping to build Falmouth and its many quays and dock installations. Flushing was the favourite home of masters of Falmouth's famous packet ships and one can see why, this being such a peaceful spot with magnificent views towards Pendennis. It was also the home of the man who was educated at the little grammar school in Truro and became Admiral Edward Pellow and then Lord Exmouth, who commanded the Mediterranean fleet in 1814. Perhaps his most famous feats were the bombing of Algiers to release slaves, and capturing the enormous ship *Cleopatra* when in

Charming buildings in the narrow streets of Flushing.

71

command of the *Nymph* with a crew of eighty Cornishmen.

Another native of Flushing was a remarkable man called Buckingham who became an author and founded a newspaper in Calcutta. When he was only eight he was involved in what might have been an ugly incident. In the 1794 famine 400 miners threatened to raid and distribute the contents of a grain ship at Flushing Quay. The master put young Buckingham on his knee while sitting on a mound of grain and commenced singing that great Methodist hymn which begins: 'Salvation, Oh the joyful sound . . .'. With caps doffed, the miners sang the hymn right through then quietly dispersed. How times have changed!

Following the road through the centre of Flushing and past the sailing club, it winds up and along to Trefusis Quay, restored by an M.S.C. scheme. From here it is only a short walk to Trefusis Point, the furthest point on our walk and with fine views across the river to Falmouth docks.

On returning to Flushing, you will see a sign indicating a path leading up to Bowling Green and a twisting lane which affords splendid views over the rooftops to the quay below. The walk is now over, apart from a cruise on the ferry back to your starting point. While waiting for it to arrive we enjoyed watching the activity on the quay. To our inexperienced eyes there appeared to be mountains of mackerel being loaded into huge lorries as 'long-liners' arrived to unload their bumper catches.

The journey back to the Prince of Wales Pier only takes a few minutes but offers unusual views of Falmouth's waterfront and new developments, a splendid finish to an interesting afternoon's walk.

The quay at Flushing.

72

Flushing and Falmouth seen over the rooftops from Bowling Green Park.

Unloading the day's catch of mackerel at Flushing Quay.

WALK TWELVE

A towpath walk alongside one of Cornwall's few
man-made waterways,
returning via high clifftops.
ALONG THE BUDE CANAL
OS Map (1:50,000) 190.
Length: approximately five and a half miles.

This is a walk combining towpath, field paths and finally coastal paths, and it takes in a tremendous variety of history and beauty. After parking your car in the main car-park, alongside the bridge below the town of Bude, take the road opposite which leads to a unique building.

Bude is connected in my mind with one of Cornwall's most colourful and brilliant scientists, Sir Goldsworthy Gurney, and his home was the castle, built right on the sandy shore. It looks just like the toy fort that I had as a child. Bude also has connections with the great Arundell family who owned the town's oldest house, Ebbingford Manor.

Finding your way to the first lock gates of the famous canal, which was officially opened in 1823, you will notice a long, stone building. This contains a Historical and Folk Exhibition of models and photographs portraying lifeboats, shipwrecks, railways and transport, natural history and geology of the area – all beautifully displayed.

Crossing the lock gates to the south of

Sir Goldsworthy Gurney's toy-like castle, built in the 1830s beside the beach.

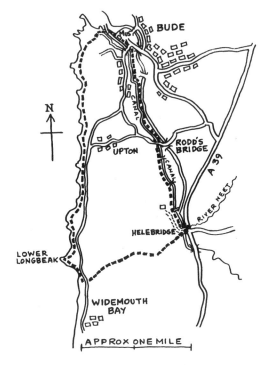

the canal, our walk now follows the towpath as far as the bridge near the car-park, where we cross to the opposite eastern bank. When originally planned, it was envisaged that the canal would be in use from the sea right up to Launceston, thirty miles away, and it was unique in that all cargo had to be transferred from barges into small tub boats at Hele Bridge, these being hauled up planes by means of either steam or water power. The cargo was mostly sand and lime, carried into the heart of the county's agricultural land to redress the mainly acid soil.

The first, broad stretch of the canal is now a safe haven for pleasure craft of all sorts and, as you journey south along the towpath, you will enjoy completely different sorts of scenery, with wild flowers in profusion and complete peace and tranquillity. We met only the occasional angler along the whole length to Hele Bridge. After crossing to the eastern bank you pass a number of old warehouses,

The canal and the river (on the right) enter the sea at almost the same point.

Anglers enjoy a quiet stretch of canal bank alongside the nature reserve.

now transformed into charming dwellings and water-sports centres. On your left, beyond a screen of willows, is the Bude Marshes Nature Reserve.

As the canal winds south through more open country, you will be unlucky if you do not see a heron flapping off as you approach, and there are numerous swans, ducks and assorted waterfowl. At Rodd's Bridge, you cross to the opposite western bank and continue south, through flatter country, until you reach Hele Bridge. Just before the bridge, cross the canal and climb up onto the main A39 road for about 100 yards, then follow the public footpath sign on the right to Widemouth which leads you through a white gate. Another 100 yards along a track, where the road curves right, follow a sign on the left and cross a stile. A path now leads south-

The final stile, where the cross-country stretch of the walk reaches Widemouth Bay.

77

After passing Chapel Rock the walk ends at the entrance to the canal.

west, up and over a hill and across fields, until you reach the coast, close to Widemouth Bay.

Turning right and following the coastal footpath north, you will soon reach Lower Longbeak, a superb vantage point for looking across Widemouth Sand and north along the rugged coast as far as the strange dish aerials near Morwenstow. On a breezy day, the walk along these high cliffs can be most exhilarating, and in spring the cliff tops are a mass of sea pinks and tiny colourful flowers.

There are several more vantage points as you walk north, and after about two miles you will reach Compass Point, where a unique octagonal hollow building gives a fine view of the pounding Atlantic surf and the jagged rocks that cause this part of the coast to be much feared. This had to be the route taken by ships approaching the lock gates of the Bude Canal, and when we were there last, we saw a flagstaff on the rock at the end of the breakwater. This is one of Cornwall's many 'chapel' rocks where, presumably, there was once a hermitage.

Rounding the point you will find yourself back at the high lock gates of the canal, the starting point of the walk. The people of Bude are lucky to have such a pleasant walk, with such a variety of scenery, right on their doorstep.

The rugged coastline to the north, as far as the cliff-top aerials near Morwenstow.

WALK THIRTEEN

A walk to mainland Britain's most southerly point,
two unspoilt fishing villages and along the top
of stout Cornish hedges.
AROUND THE LIZARD
OS Map (1:50,000) 203 and 204.
Length: approximately two, four and a half or seven miles.

Until recently our family group had members ranging in age between eighty-nine and five, yet we still managed to have days out walking together, some taking the longer route, others taking a shorter walk, but all finishing at the same point. One such walk is that from the village of Lizard. It can vary in length from two miles to seven miles, depending on one's abilities and the state of the weather.

Leaving your car in the village car-park, head due west, past the public toilets and craft workshops and past a 'No Through Road' sign down to Caerthillian Cove. From here the path climbs steeply up to the clifftop, leading south past Holseer Cove to Lizard Point. The view from this vantage point across the width of Mount's Bay is magnificent. On a clear afternoon you can look right across to Gwennap Head, over twenty miles away.

Now we walk west along the clifftop of springy turf and wild flowers to Polpeor Cove. The path descends to a small wooden bridge before climbing above the old Lizard lifeboat station to the most southerly point on the British mainland, with its cafés and souvenir shops. The density of traffic out at sea off the Lizard is quite high, not quite frenetic but very busy, and comprises every sort and size of vessel. Before continuing round the coast you may wish to descend the slipway to the old lifeboat station and admire masses of wild mesembryanthemum clinging to the cliffs. The last time I visited the Lizard, most eyes were diverted from the passing ships to a seal which was playing in the surf at the foot of the cliffs, near the rocks of Vellan Drang.

The old Lizard lifeboat house at the foot of mesembryanthemum-clad cliffs.

If you wish to limit your walk to just two miles, then follow the path up past the cafés to the village and car-park. To continue the walk, head east again, passing beneath the Lizard lighthouse, built in 1751 by Sir John Killigrew on the site of an even older construction. I am reminded of a terrified little daughter leaping into my arms when years ago we were walking beside this lighthouse when its foghorn started up. Father was startled too!

The path now curves north-east into Housel Bay. The path sometimes meanders very close to the cliff edge, so be warned and keep dogs and small children on a 'short rein'. What a wealth of lovely names the map gives at this point: Lion's Den, Enoch Rock, Bumble Rock. At the centre of the bay, the path passes above the clean white sand of Housel Cove before descending steeply. A path to the left leads up to the famous Housel Bay Hotel, a good place to enjoy a mid-walk meal, while you look out to sea where a rock so like a sitting cat can be seen. The path to the right climbs slowly to Pen Olver and round to the coastguard lookout on Bass Point.

The new lifeboat station at Kilcobben Cove.

Now we begin to head roughly north, following the coastal footpath to Kilcobben Cove, the new site for the Lizard lifeboat, with its funicular railway down the steep cliffside from the road to the boathouse. The difference between this sheltered site and the stormy position of its previous base is quite remarkable.

Around the headland to the north is Church Cove, a narrow inlet with a steep slipway up which fishing boats are hauled out of the way of winter storms. An old 'pilchard palace' has been beautifully converted into a private dwelling here. If your legs are beginning to feel the strain, a

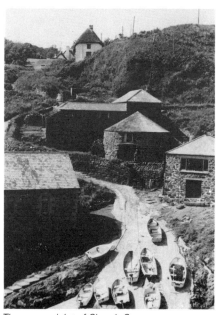

The narrow inlet of Church Cove.

80

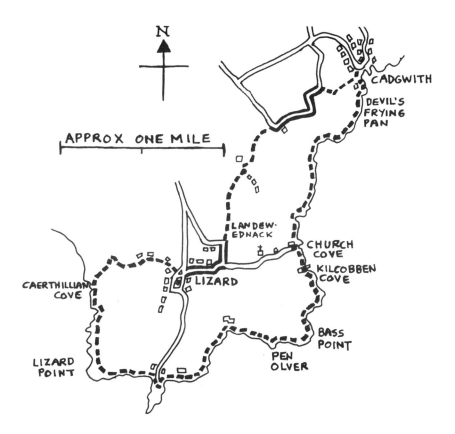

An old fish 'palace' converted into a private dwelling at Church Cove.

road winds up past delightful thatched cottages, back to your car, making a walk of roughly four and a half miles. En route you pass the church at Landewednack, idyllically sited in a shallow valley alongside more thatched cottages.

For those brave souls wishing to extend their walk from Church Cove itself, the coastal path continues north along the clifftop, dipping inland on several occasions. Passing the coves and headlands of Polbarrow, Polgwidden, Chough's Ogo and Dollar Ogo, we come to the Devil's Frying Pan, a strange natural phenomenon of a deep hollow scooped out of the cliff

The Devil's Frying Pan, where water surges at high tide.

and filled with water at all but low tide. The path now descends between pretty gardens to Cadgwith and what must be Cornwall's most unspoilt fishing village.

Picturesque it may be, but it also has a most honourble and proud history of bravery within the embrace of the R.N.L.I. I was told that the old lifeboat saved over 200 lives in one incident alone! If you forewent a meal at the Housel Bay Hotel, you may be glad of a delicious crab salad at Sharkey Stephen's café in a converted fish cellar.

Instead of returning to Lizard along the coastal footpath, a pleasant walk is to follow the old footpaths inland. From Cadgwith, climb the steep road out of the village to the south and then take one of several tracks heading south-west to Prazegooth where you join a minor road. Follow this until, just past Gwavas Farm, the road turns northwest. At this point you follow a footpath across the fields heading southwest to Trethvas Farm and Lizard. It must be one of the most unusual footpaths in Cornwall since it runs along the top of several Cornish hedges – doubly thick, of course.

Just south of Trethvas Farm, take the wall to the right, which leads you to Cross Common and Lizard. The wall to the left takes you back down to Landewednack Church. These wall-walkways must have been very practical for communication between villages during heavy snowfall.

Part of the hedgetop footpath leading back across the fields to Lizard.

Fishermen's lofts and houses cluster round the shingle beach at Cadgwith.

WALK FOURTEEN

A country walk along the upper reaches of one of Cornwall's most beautiful rivers.
ALONG THE CAMEL TO ADVENT CHURCH
OS Map (1:50,000) 200.
Length: approximately three miles.

This is a walk into real countryside, so your rucksack should contain a picnic or something to eat for there will certainly be nowhere to call for a 'bar snack' or the like. Leave your car in the car-park between the river and the parish church in Camelford and walk back over the bridge and past the town hall, which appropriately has a camel on its weather-vane.

This is one of Cornwall's ancient towns and it had a market as far back as the thirteenth century. In spite of its busy shopping street it still retains its dignified air of antiquity and many old buildings. Make your way for a short distance along Fore Street until you find an unusual footpath sign on your left marked 'To River and Advent Church', beside a passage just

A camel weather-vane surmounts the town hall at Camelford.

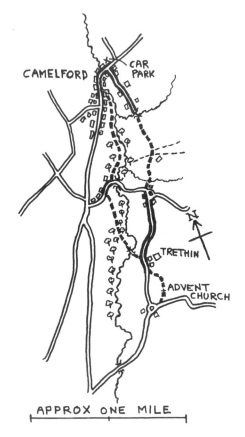

CAMELFORD · CAR PARK · TRETHIN · ADVENT CHURCH

APPROX ONE MILE

beyond the shoe shop. Pass through and within a couple of hundred yards you have left the bustle of a busy market town and the sound of traffic and find yourself walking beside the River Camel, with water meadows on the far bank.

The riverside walk for the next quarter of a mile is very picturesque, with the river meandering through flat meadows and tall trees to your right. I recall a most dramatic sight a few miles downstream, just below Grogley Halt, a few years ago. Several hundred sea trout and mullet had come upstream on a spring tide – a miniature Bristol Avon bore – and were feeding on the surface of the water.

We have done this walk in very muddy and wet conditions, especially near the series of kissing gates and stiles that lead you to Fenteroon Bridge, but careful stepping and stout boots should combat this hazard. On reaching the old granite bridge, which carries a minor road over the River Camel, turn right and walk up the hill.

On reaching the second gate on the left you will see another footpath sign pointing to the prettiest part of the walk, especially in late spring when primroses and bluebells are in bloom. Cross two fields

The young River Camel meanders through flat meadows.

The first of five bridges encountered during this walk.

In mid-summer the surrounding greenery is almost sub-tropical.

Fenteroon Bridge, composed of large granite slabs.

and a stile and the path suddenly plunges into a delightful wood and downhill to the water meadows again. A little footbridge leads to an idyllic setting for a picnic. Surely it would be difficult to find a more serene and beautiful place to sit quietly beside the river and let nature's music of water and bird, sheep and rook, soothe away the ugliness we all have to endure at times.

Suitably refreshed, climb steeply up across a field and into a lane, passing Trethin Holiday Farm. You are now nearing Advent Church, which can be reached by two routes. If the ground underfoot is not too wet, take the footpath just past the farm which leads up across a couple of fields to the church. But if this proves too soggy underfoot, continue along the road to the hamlet of Tresinney and turn left, taking a short track to the church.

When we first saw this church, it appeared to stand alone and rather defiantly in the middle of a field without any apparent path leading to it. It is mainly fifteenth-century and in common with many Cornish churches it contains a Norman font. If you look up at the middle of the ancient roof you will see carved human faces whose eyes appear to follow as you walk around the interior. Perhaps this and Temple Church on Bodmin Moor are the loneliest churches I know.

This is such a beautiful walk that one might wish to return by the same path, but to vary it, walk back as far as Trethin Farm and continue along the narrow lane as far as the pretty little hamlet of Pencarrow. Walking straight ahead, just to the left of a farm building, you will see a footpath leading down across a field (diagonally to the right) to a single-plank bridge across a

An idyllic spot for a picnic.

stream. The footpath now climbs to the farmhouse of Treclago and follows a track for a short distance before striking off north, crossing several fields and descending to Outground Mill. After crossing a small footbridge, the path now reaches a narrow road which leads back, past Highermead Park Hotel, into the centre of Camelford.

My wife and I count this as our favourite riverside walk, and others think it is the most attractive route to reach Rough Tor and the high parts of Bodmin Moor.

We hope that you enjoy this, as well as the other suggested walks in this book.

Advent Church on its hilltop site.

The waterfall and pool below a precarious single-plank bridge.

The quiet interior of the Church of St Athwenna, dating from the fifteenth century.

The
WALKING CORNWALL
series
Donald Vage

Donald Vage made a name for himself through his series of walks that first appeared in Cornish Life magazine and, later, on Radio Cornwall.

The three books that go to make up the Walking Cornwall series have been immensely popular, providing a glimpse of Cornwall through the eyes of one who knows the county intimately - and who, with his wife, has walked many of Cornwall's byeways.

BOOK 1
Ten Cornish Coastal and Countryside Walks

BOOK 2
Fourteen Cornish Coastal and Countryside Walks
including the Saint's Way

BOOK 3
Fourteen Cornish Countryside, Moorland and
Coastal Walks

The Walking Cornwall series is available from all good bookshops, or direct from the publisher.

Exploring the deep winding lanes of Cornwall, the quiet creeks, peaceful moorland heights, wooded river banks, tors and waterfalls, hamlets, villages and churches of his native county has long been a favourite pastime of Truro jeweller Donald Vage. His popular broadcasts on BBC Radio Cornwall and monthly features in *Cornish Life Magazine* have already tempted many people to explore some of the lesser-known areas of their county. In his first book Donald Vage gathered together ten of his favourite coastal and countryside walks in Cornwall. Now, Book Two will fascinate with fourteen more. Both books are illustrated with maps and photographs. Many of the walks are as well suited to the elderly or disabled as to the young and active.

CORNWALL BOOKS

Cornwall Books is an imprint of Westcountry Books which publishes a wide range of titles covering the South West, from walks books to full colourphotographic books of the region's landscape and people.

A full catalogue of the 150 titles now available is free on request from:

Westcountry Books
Unit 1 Chinon Court
Lower Moor Way
Tiverton
Devon EX16 6SS

Tel: 0884 243242
Fax: 0884 243325

WESTCOUNTRY BOOKS

PUBLISHING UNDER THE FOLLOWING IMPRINTS

BADGER BOOKS   CORNWALL BOOKS   DEVON BOOKS   DORSET BOOKS

EXMOOR BOOKS   EXMOOR PRESS   HALSGROVE PRESS   WESTCOUNTRY BOOKS